Ten Little Fingers

100 number rhymes for young children

Louise Binder Scott

Cover illustration by
Tim Foley

Inside illustrations by
Teena Hahn

LDA

Copyright Notice

All finger plays and rhymes in this book are the author's
original contributions unless specified otherwise.

Dedication
In loving memory of Louise Binder Scott
whose delightful action rhymes and finger plays
truly entertain young children

Ten Little Fingers
MT00452
ISBN-10: 85503 274 0
ISBN-13: 978 1 85503 274 3
© LDA
All rights reserved
First published 1999.
Reprinted 2000, 2001, 2002, 2003, 2005, 2006, 2009
Printed in the UK for LDA

LDA Pintail Close, Victoria Business Park,
Nottingham, NG4 2SG UK

Table of Contents

Finger plays and action rhymes have descended through the ages and are found in most countries of the world. Their perpetuation appears to be due to the physical and close contact of the parent-child relationships in which the family is involved. To the parent, finger plays are a way of helping the child move toward self-discovery and mastery over the movements of his fingers, hands, and arms. To the teacher, finger plays have many additional values. The manual dexterity and muscular control acquired in the earlier finger games played with the parent can be utilized and expanded into an understanding of rhythm—the rhythm of speech and music, the rhythm of life's activities.

Teaching finger plays and action rhymes requires a number of simple techniques. Although each "game" has certain individual elements, the following list of suggestions will help the teacher in presenting the rhymes.

1. If you are facing the child or a group of children, you should mirror the actions which you wish the child to perform. For example, if you wish the child to use her right hand, you should hold up your left hand. Children will tend to move in the same direction as the demonstrator facing them. The teacher, then, must make her movements in the reverse of those expected from the group.

2. Be aware, too, of the fact that there may be children in the group who are left-handed. These children may perform certain right-handed movements in an awkward manner. If you sense a coordination problem, suggest to the child that s/he, too, face the class.

3. Get the children to follow just the actions until they understand what they are to do during the rhyme or finger play. After they have played the "game" once, they will be able to say a few of the words after you.

4. Repeat each finger play several times before going on to another. Children will need to repeat the rhyme in order to learn it. As the rhyme becomes more familiar, children will ask to do it over and over again.

5. Have fun with these rhymes and the children will respond to your enthusiasm.

Swinging birds

Two tall telephone poles,
(Hold up hands, palms inward,
index finger erect.)
Across them a wire is strung;
(Extend middle fingers until they touch at tips.)
Two little birds hopped on,
(Move thumbs to touch extended middle fingers.)
And swung and swung and swung.
(Swing hands back and forth.)
—Traditional

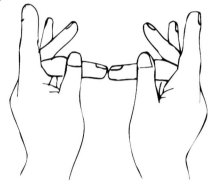

Seven plump robins

Seven plump robins were hopping all around,
Picking up bread crumbs off the ground.
Two saw a yellow cat up in a tree.
Two flew away, then there were three!
One heard a black cat say, "Mew, Mew,"
He flew away, then there were two.
One saw a striped cat sitting in the sun.
One saw a white cat and she began to run.
Now there were no robins hopping all around,
Picking up bread crumbs off the ground.
(Show the designated number of fingers each time.
Children may supply the number remaining.)

Five little robins

Five little robins in a sycamore tree,
A father,
   (Hold up thumb.)
A mother,
   (Hold up index finger.)
And babies three;
   (Hold up remaining fingers.)
Father brought a worm,
   (Point to thumb.)
Mother brought a bug;
   (Point to index finger.)
The three baby robins started to tug;
This one ate the bug,
   (Point to middle finger.)
This one ate the worm,
   (Point to ring finger.)
And this one sat and waited for his turn.
   (Point to little finger.)

Five little bunnies

Five little bunnies are such dears!
The first little bunny has pink ears.
   (Hold up a finger at each side of head.)
The second little bunny has soft toes.
   (Point to feet.)
The third little bunny sniffs with her nose.
   (Make two sniffs.)
The fourth little bunny is very smart.
   (Point to forehead.)
The fifth little bunny has a loving heart.
   (Place hand over heart.)

(This rhyme can be used as a finger play or acted out.)

Twelve little rabbits

Twelve little rabbits in a rabbit pen;
Two hopped away and then there were ten.
   (Hold up ten fingers.)
Ten little rabbits with ears up straight;
Two hopped away and then there were eight.
   (Bend down two fingers.)
Eight little rabbits doing funny tricks;
Two hopped away and then there were six.
   (Bend down two fingers.)
Six little rabbits eating carrots from the store;
Two hopped away and then there were four.
   (Bend down two fingers.)
Four little rabbits looked for gardens new;
Two hopped away and then there were two.
   (Bend down two fingers.)
Two little rabbits found a new friend;
They hopped away, and that is the end.
   (Bend down last two fingers.)

Ten huge dinosaurs

Ten huge dinosaurs were standing in a line.
One tripped on a cobblestone and then there were _____.

Nine huge dinosaurs were trying hard to skate.
One cracked right through the ice, and then there were _____.

Eight huge dinosaurs were counting past eleven.
One counted up too far, and then there were _____.

Seven huge dinosaurs learned some magic tricks,
One did a disappearing act, and then there were _____.

Six huge dinosaurs were learning how to drive.
One forgot the petrol, and so then there were _____.

Five huge dinosaurs joined the drum corps.
One forgot the drumsticks, and then there were _____.

Four huge dinosaurs were wading in the sea.
One waded too far out, and then there were _____.

Three huge dinosaurs waiting in a queue.
One got bored and left, and then there were _____.

Two huge dinosaurs went to the Amazon.
One sailed in up to his head, and then there was _____.

One lonesome dinosaur knew his friends had gone.
He found a big museum, and then there were _____.
    —Adapted from an old English rhyme

(Children may supply the number remaining.)

Five little owls

This little owl has great, round eyes.
This little owl is a very small size.
This little owl can turn her head.
This little owl likes mice, she said.
This little owl flies all around,
And her wings make hardly a single sound.
(Point to one finger at a time.)

Dive, little tadpole

Dive, little tadpole, one;
    (Hold up one finger.)
Dive, little tadpoles, two;
    (Hold up two fingers.)
Swim, little tadpoles, Oh, oh, oh!
    (Clap three times.)
Or I will catch YOU!
    (Point.)

Five little squirrels

Five little squirrels lived up in a tree.
    (Hold up five fingers.)
And they were alike as squirrels could be.
The first little squirrel was alone one day.
    (Point to one finger at a time.)
He called to his friends, "Come on and play!"
The second little squirrel jumped down from a limb.
The first little squirrel jumped after him.
The third little squirrel found nuts to eat.
He cracked them and oh, they tasted sweet.
The fourth little squirrel played hide and seek.
She hid her eyes and she did not peek.
The fifth little squirrel called, "Chirr-chirr-chirr-eee,"
And all of the squirrels came back to the tree.
    (Hold up five fingers.)

Ten little froggies

Ten little froggies were swimming in a pool.
   (Hold up ten fingers.)
This little froggie said, "Let's go to school!"
   (Point to thumb.)
This little froggie said, "Oh, yes! Let's go!"
   (Point to index finger.)
This little froggie said, "We'll sit in a row."
   (Point to middle finger.)
This little froggie said, "We'll learn to read."
   (Point to ring finger.)
This little froggie said, "Yes, yes, indeed."
   (Point to little finger.)
This little froggie said, "We'll learn to write."
   (Point to thumb on other hand.)
This little froggie said, "We'll try with all our might."
   (Point to index finger.)
This little froggie said, "We will draw and sing."
   (Point to middle finger.)
This little froggie said, "We'll learn EVERYTHING!"
   (Point to ring finger.)
This little froggie said, "Then after school,
   (Point to little finger.)
We'll come back here and swim in our pool."
   (Make swimming motions with fingers.)

Where are the baby mice?

Where are the baby mice?
Squeak, squeak, squeak!
   (Make fist and hide it behind you.)
I cannot see them;
Peek, peek, peek!
   (Show fist and extend it.)
Here they come out of their hole in the wall.
One, two, three, four, five, and that is all!
   (Show one finger at a time.)

The adventures of little mice

Five little mice looked for something to eat.
They wanted to have a wonderful treat.
The first little mouse nibbled at a slice
Of warm, fresh bread and it tasted nice.
The second little mouse nibbled at a cake.
He ate fast and got a tummy ache.
The third little mouse nibbled at a pie.
It tasted sweet and she gave a sigh.
The fourth little mouse nibbled at some cheese.
The fifth little mouse said, "Be quiet, please.
I hear someone coming to open the door!"
So they all hid under a board in the floor.
   (Five children dramatize the rhyme. It can be used
   as a finger play; point to one finger at a time.)

Five little mice

Five little mice on the pantry floor;
    (Hold up five fingers.)
This little mouse peeked behind the door;
    (Bend down little finger.)
This little mouse nibbled at the cake;
    (Bend down ring finger.)
This little mouse not a sound did make;
    (Bend down middle finger.)
This little mouse took a bite of cheese;
    (Bend down index finger.)
This little mouse heard the kitten sneeze.
    (Bend down thumb.)
"Ah-choo!" sneezed Kitten, and "Squeak!" they cried,
As they found a hole and ran inside.
    (Make running motion with fingers
    and hide hand behind back.)

The animals

I saw one hungry little mouse.
Squeak, squeak, squeak!
I said, "There's cheese inside my house."
Squeak, squeak, squeak!
I saw two funny little moles.
Creep, creep, creep!
I said, "I'll help you dig your holes
Deep, deep, deep!"
I saw three frogs beside three logs.
Glug, glug, glug!
I fed some bugs to the hungry frogs.
Glug, glug, glug!
Four little fish swam with a swish.
Glip, glip, glup!
I fed some seaweed to the fish.
Glip, glip, glup!
I said, "Here rabbits, come and eat."
Nibble, nibble, nibble.
I fed five rabbits carrots sweet.
Nibble, nibble, nibble.
Six butterflies said, "Come and fly."
Flutter, flutter, fly!
I went to fly with the butterflies.
Flutter, flutter, fly!
(Children show designated number
of fingers and say the animal's
sound or refrain.)

Five little bears

Five little bears were sitting on the ground.
   (Five children sit in a row.)
Five little bears made a deep growling sound:
Grrrrrr!
   (Children growl.)
The first one said, "Let's have a look around."
   (One child at a time rises.)
The second one said, "I feel rather funny!"
The third one said, "I think I smell honey."
The fourth one said "Shall we climb up the tree?"
The fifth one said, "Look out! There's a bee!"
So the five little bears went back to their play,
   (Children return to seats.)
And decided to wait till the bees flew away.

Elephants

One baby elephant was playing in the sun.
   (Child walks around ring.)
He thought that playing was such a lot of fun,
He called another elephant and asked him to come.
   (A second child joins first.)
Two baby elephants were playing in the sun.
They thought that playing was such a lot of fun,
They called another elephant and asked her to come.
   (A third child joins in.)
Three baby elephants were playing in the sun.
They thought that playing was such a lot of fun,
They called another elephant and asked him to come.
   (A fourth appears.)
   (Continue the game, adding more children until ten
   are participating. End the rhyme in this way:)
Ten baby elephants were playing in the sun.
They thought that playing was such a lot of fun,
They didn't call another elephant to come.
   —*A traditional English rhyme*
   (Choose ten more children, so each will have a turn.)

Counting at the zoo

Count one, 1.
Come and have some fun!
Count two, 1, 2.
Let's run to the zoo!
Count three, 1, 2, 3.
A monkey's in a tree.
Count four, 1, 2, 3, 4.
Hear the animals roar.
Count five, 1, 2, 3, 4, 5.
Watch the porpoise dive.
Count six, 1, 2, 3, 4, 5, 6.
An ape is doing tricks.
Count seven, 1, 2, 3, 4, 5, 6, 7.
The giraffe is high as heaven.

(As a finger play: point to a finger each time when counting. Suggest that the children add other animals to the zoo or substitute lines such as: "Hear the lion roar," "See the whooping crane stand in the rain," "See the big old moose. He must not get loose," "See the polar bear with white and furry hair.")

Fun at the zoo

One, one; the zoo is lots of fun!
   (Hold up hands with fingers extended;
   bend down one finger.)
Two, two; see a kangaroo!
   (Bend down one finger.)
Three, three; see a chimpanzee!
   (Bend down one finger.)
Four, four; hear the lions roar!
   (Bend down one finger.)
Five, five; watch the seal dive!
   (Bend down one finger.)
Six, six; there's a monkey doing tricks!
   (Bend down one finger.)
Seven, seven; elephants eleven!
   (Bend down one finger.)
Eight, eight; a tiger and his mate!
   (Bend down one finger.)
Nine, nine; penguins in a line!
   (Bend down one finger.)
Ten, ten; I want to come again!
   (Bend down one finger; then clap hands.)

The birthday child

A birthday child had a birthday cake
With five candles burning bright.
(Hold up five fingers.)
She blew out two of the candles,
How many still had light?
(Hold up three fingers.)
How old is the birthday child? Do you know?
She is five years old. She told me so!
(Hold up five fingers.)
(Change the word "five" to "six"
as appropriate.)

Four or five candles

Two candles,
(Hold up two fingers on left hand.)
Two candles,
(Hold up two fingers on right hand.)
That makes four.
I cannot see any more.
Four pretty candles, all the same—
Blow them out to play this game!
One *(blow)*, two *(blow)*, three *(blow)*, and four *(blow)*.
(Blow on fingers as if blowing out candles.)
Are they all gone? Are there more?
Oh, yes, I see another one.
(Hold up one finger.)
That makes five for birthday fun!
(Hold up five fingers.)
Five pretty candles, all the same—
Blow them out to play this game!

My birthday cake

My birthday cake is _____ (*any colour*) and white;
   (*Make a circle with arms.*)
The lighted candles make it bright;
1, 2, 3, 4, 5 pink candles!
   (*Hold up fingers one by one to represent candles.*)
What a pretty sight!
   (*Change the number of candles to correspond
   with child's age.*)

Six little candles

Six little candles on a birthday cake;
     (*Hold up six fingers.*)
The flames look so alive.
You may blow one candle out!
Wh! And that leaves five!
     (*Bend down one finger.*)

Five little candles on a birthday cake;
     (*Hold up five fingers.*)
Just five, and not one more.
You may blow one candle out!
Wh! And that leaves four!
     (*Bend down one finger.*)

Four little candles on a birthday cake;
     (*Hold up four fingers.*)
As bright as they could be.
You may blow one candle out!
Wh! And that leaves three!
     (*Bend down one finger.*)

Three little candles on a birthday cake;
     (*Hold up three fingers.*)
Standing straight and true.
You may blow one candle out!
Wh! And that leaves two!
     (*Bend down one finger.*)

Two little candles on a birthday cake;
     (*Hold up two fingers.*)
Helping us have fun.
You may blow one candle out!
Wh! And that leaves one!
     (*Bend down one finger.*)

One little candle on a birthday cake;
It knows its job is done.
You may blow this candle out!
Wh! And that leaves none!
     (*Place hands behind back.*)

*("Wh" is a two-letter consonant speech sound which appears
in such words as white, what, when, and where.)*

Ten circus wagons

Ten circus wagons, painted oh, so bright,
Came into town with the circus last night!
(Hold up ten fingers.)
This one holds a lion
That gives a big, loud roar!
(Point to thumb on opposite hand.)
This one holds a tiger
Fast asleep upon the floor.
(Point to index finger.)
This one holds a funny seal
That nods to left and right.
(Point to middle finger.)
This one holds a zebra
That is striped all black and white.
(Point to ring finger.)
This one holds a camel
With two humps upon his back.
(Point to little finger.)

This one holds a panther
With his coat of fur so black.
(Point to thumb on other hand.)
This one holds an elephant
That is drinking from a pail.
(Point to index finger.)
This one holds a monkey
That is swinging by his tail.
(Point to middle finger.)
This one holds a hippo
With a grin so very wide.
(Point to ring finger.)
This one holds a leopard
With a very spotty hide.
(Point to little finger.)
Ten circus wagons, painted oh, so bright,
Came into town with the circus last night!
(Hold up ten fingers.)

One finger, two

One finger, two fingers,
  (Pop up little and ring fingers.)
Belong just to me.
Up pops a third one,
  (Pop up middle finger.)
Now there are three.
Up pops a fourth one,
  (Pop up index finger.)
Now there are four.
Up pops your thumb,
  (Pop up thumb.)
Let's do it once more.

I see three

I see three—one, two, three,
  (Hold up three fingers one at a time.)
  Three little mice
  Playing with a dice.
I see three—one, two, three,
  (Bend down three fingers one at a time.)
  Three little kittens
  All wearing mittens.
I see three—one, two, three,
  (Hold up three fingers one at a time.)
  Three little frogs
  Sitting on logs.
I see three—one, two, three,
  (Bend down three fingers one at a time.)
  Three little bears
  Climbing upstairs.
I see three—one, two, three,
  (Hold up three fingers one at a time.)
  Three little ducks
  Riding on trucks.

Five came out to play

Five little bugs came out to play.

1, 2, 3, 4, 5!

(Pop up fingers one at a time.)

They spied a bird and they ran away.

5, 4, 3, 2, 1!

(Bend down fingers one at a time.)

Five little birds came out for some air.

1, 2, 3, 4, 5!

They saw a cat and they flew out of there.

5, 4, 3, 2, 1!

Five little cats went out to the park.

1, 2, 3, 4, 5!

They saw a dog and were scared of his bark.

5, 4, 3, 2, 1!

Five little dogs heard a donkey cough.

1, 2, 3, 4, 5!

They turned on their tails and they scampered off.

5, 4, 3, 2, 1!

Six donkeys hid behind the trees,

(Hold hands behind back.)

When they heard the buzz of a swarm of bees.

Learning to count

One, one; now we have begun;
   (Hold up one finger.)
Two, two; shoes that are new;
   (Hold up two fingers.)
Three, three; birds in a tree;
   (Hold up three fingers.)
Four, four; blocks on the floor;
   (Hold up four fingers.)
Five, five; bees in a hive;
   (Hold up five fingers.)
Six, six; little drumsticks;
   (Hold up six fingers.)
Seven, seven; clouds in the heaven;
   (Hold up seven fingers.)
Eight, eight; cookies on a plate;
   (Hold up eight fingers.)
Nine, nine; grapes on a vine;
   (Hold up nine fingers.)
Ten, ten; let's all count again;
   (Hold up ten fingers.)
1, 2, 3, 4, 5, 6, 7, 8, 9, 10.
   (Bend fingers down one by one.)

Captain and men

1, 2, 3, 4, 5 in a row.
   (Pop up fingers one at a time on right hand.)
A Captain and his men!
And on the other side, you know,
Are 6, 7, 8, 9, and 10.
   (Pop up fingers one at a time on left hand.)

One, two, how do you do?

1, 2, how do you do?
1, 2, 3, clap with me;
1, 2, 3, 4, jump on the floor;
1, 2, 3, 4, 5, look bright and alive;
1, 2, 3, 4, 5, 6, your shoe to fix;
1, 2, 3, 4, 5, 6, 7, look up to heaven;
1, 2, 3, 4, 5, 6, 7, 8, draw a round plate;
1, 2, 3, 4, 5, 6, 7, 8, 9, get in line!
   (Point to one finger at a time.)

Counting action rhyme

One, two; sit up. Please do!
   (Children sit up straight.)
Three, four; feet flat on the floor.
   (Feet on floor.)
Five, six; stir and mix.
   (Motion of stirring.)
Seven, eight; close the gate.
   (Clap.)
Nine, ten; make a pen for a hen.
   (Interlace fingers.)

Dive little goldfish

Dive, little goldfish one.
   (Hold up one finger.)
Dive little goldfish two.
   (Hold up two fingers.)
Dive, little goldfish three—
   (Hold up three fingers.)
Here is food, you see!
   (Sprinkling motion with fingers.)
Dive, little goldfish four.
   (Hold up four fingers.)
Dive, little goldfish five.
   (Hold up five fingers.)
Dive, little goldfish six—
   (Hold up six fingers.)
I like your funny tricks.

My family

Here is my lovely mother;
(Point to index finger.)
Here is my father tall;
(Point to middle finger.)
Here is my older brother,
(Point to ring finger.)
And that isn't all;
Here is my baby brother,
(Point to little finger.)
As small as small can be.
Who is this other person?
(Point to thumb.)
Why, of course, it's ME!
1, 2, 3, 4, 5, you see,
(Touch each finger as you count.)
Make a very nice family!

Counting at the farm

One, one. A farm is lots of fun.
(Hold up thumb.)
Two, two. Hear the kitten mew.
(Hold up two fingers.)
Three, three. Birds are in a tree.
(Hold up three fingers.)
Four, four. Hear the puppy snore.
(Hold up four fingers.)
Five, five. Bees buzz in a hive.
(Hold up thumb and all fingers.)

Farmer Jones' farm

One dog,
Two cats,
Three goats,
And four white rats.
Five hens,
Six cows,
Seven geese,
And eight sows.
Nine sheep,
Ten lambs,
And hidden away where nobody sees,
Are a hundred and fifty honey bees!
(The children hold up the required number of fingers each time.)

Five little chickens

Five little chickens by the old barn door;
    (Hold up five fingers.)
One saw a beetle, and then there were four.
    (Bend down one finger.)
Four little chickens under a tree;
One saw a cricket, and then there were three.
    (Bend down one finger.)
Three little chickens looked for something new;
One saw a grasshopper; then there were two.
    (Bend down one finger.)
Two little chickens said, "Oh, what fun!"
One saw a ladybird; then there was one.
    (Bend down one finger.)
One little chicken began to run,
For he saw a sly old fox; then there were none!
    (Bend down one finger.)

Ten fluffy chickens

Five eggs and five eggs,
    (Hold up two hands.)
That makes ten;
Sitting on top is Mother Hen.
    (Clap three times.)
What do I see?
Ten fluffy chickens
    (Hold up ten fingers.)
As yellow as can be!

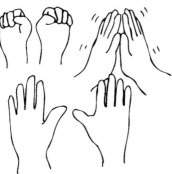

Ten little ducklings

Ten little ducklings,
    (Move hands back and forth
    in waddling motion.)
Dash, dash, dash!
Jumped in the duck pond,
    (Motion of jumping.)
Splash, splash, splash!
When the mother called them,
"Quack, quack, quack,"
Ten little ducklings
    (Hold up ten fingers.)
Swam right back.
    (Motion of swimming.)

Five little goslings

One little gosling, yellow and new,
   (Hold up one finger.)
Had a fuzzy brother, and that made two.
   (Hold up two fingers.)
Two little goslings now you can see;
They had a little sister, and that made three.
   (Hold up three fingers.)
Three little goslings waddled through the door;
Another sister got in line, and that made four.
   (Hold up four fingers.)
Four little goslings went to swim and dive;
They met a little neighbour, and that made five.
   (Hold up five fingers.)
Five little goslings; watch them grow!
   (Spread hands wide apart.)
They'll turn into fine, big geese, you know!
   (The word gosling may be changed to "duckling.")

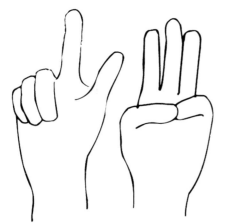

The goose family

Mr. Gander and Mrs. Goose,
   *(Hold up thumb and index finger on one
   hand.)*
And their goslings, one, two, three,
   (Hold up other three fingers on other hand.)
Are two and three, which make, you see,
A happy family.
Said Mr. Gander to Mrs. Goose,
   (Bend down thumb and index finger.)
"The water's fine, I see;
We'll both go swimming, you and I,
With our babies, one, two, three."
   (Bend down other three fingers.)

Five little pussy cats

Five little pussy cats;
  (Hold up five fingers.)
See them play!
  (Wiggle fingers.)
This one is brown,
  (Bend down thumb.)
And this one is grey;
  (Bend down index finger.)
This one has a white nose;
  (Bend down middle finger.)
This one has sharp claws;
  (Bend down ring finger.)
This one has long whiskers
  (Bend down little finger.)
And tiny, soft paws.
1, 2, 3, 4, 5 pussy cats,
  (Pop up fingers as you count.)
Hurry away to scare the mice and rats.
  (Wiggle fingers.)
SQUEAK!
  (Clap hands.)
    —Adapted

Four billy goats

The first billy goat climbs on the roof.
The second billy goat taps with his hoof.
The third billy goat doesn't want to wait.
The fourth billy goat opens up the gate.
Four billy goats get into the garden
And don't even say, "I beg your pardon."
  (Point to one finger at a time.)

Frisky little ponies

One little pony so full of fun
  (Hold up one finger.)
Likes to whinny and trot and run.
Two little ponies eat oats from a trough.
  (Hold up two fingers.)
And when they are full, they gallop off.
Three little ponies like their snacks
  (Hold up three fingers.)
Before they will give us rides on their backs.

Six young roosters

Six young roosters began to play;
When all of a sudden, one ran away.
Five young roosters began to crow;
When all of a sudden, one hurt his toe.
Four young roosters went to the fair;
When all of a sudden, one wasn't there.
Three young roosters, and just as I feared;
All of a sudden, one disappeared!
Two young roosters pecked on the ground;
When all of a sudden, one couldn't be found.
One young rooster went to his nest;
When all of a sudden, he found all the rest.

*(Ask for volunteers to play the six
roosters. They sit on a rug representing
a set. One at a time leaves and at the
end all return. All say the line "When
all of a sudden," until they are more
familiar with the rhyme.)*

In my little garden

In my little garden with a lovely view,
Sunflowers are smiling, one and two.
In my little garden by the apple tree,
Daffodils are dancing, one, two, three.
In my little garden by the kitchen door,
Roses now are blooming, one, two, three, four.
In my little garden by the winding drive,
Violets are growing, one, two, three, four, five.
   *(The children hold up required
   number of fingers each time.)*

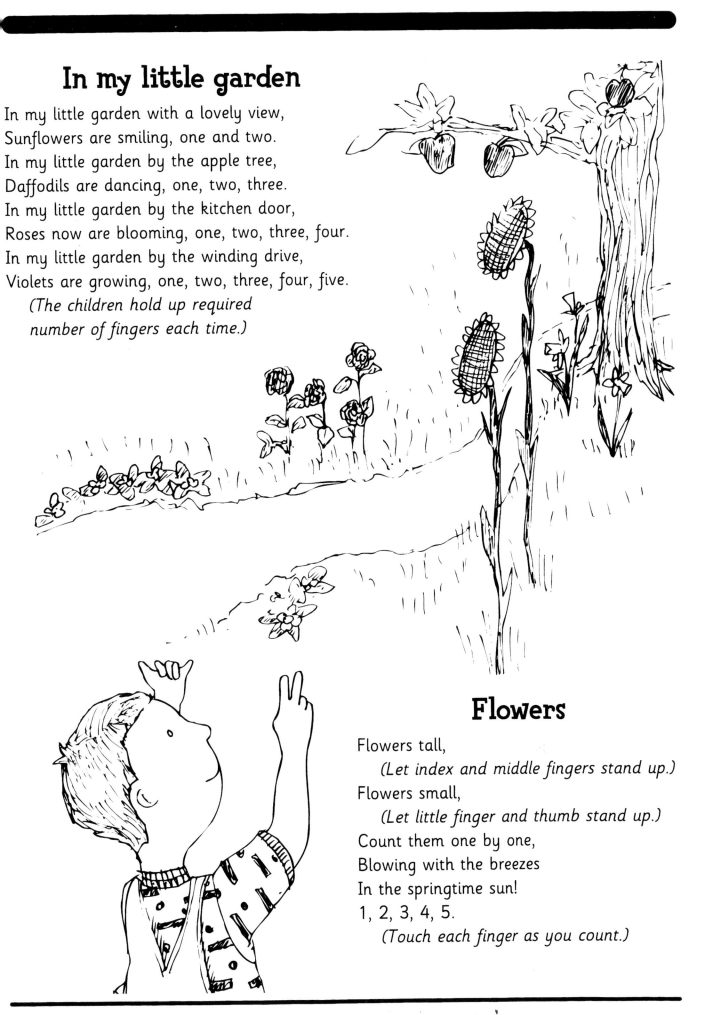

Flowers

Flowers tall,
   (Let index and middle fingers stand up.)
Flowers small,
   (Let little finger and thumb stand up.)
Count them one by one,
Blowing with the breezes
In the springtime sun!
1, 2, 3, 4, 5.
   (Touch each finger as you count.)

Things that grow

Here is my little garden bed.
Here is one tomato ripe and red.
Here are two great, long string beans.
Here are three bunches of spinach greens.
Here are four cucumbers on a vine.
This little garden is all mine.

(Hold up designated number of fingers.)

Relaxing flowers

Five little flowers
Standing in the sun;
(Hold up five fingers.)
See their heads nodding,
Bowing, one by one.
(Bend fingers several times.)
Down, down, down
Comes the gentle rain,
(Raise hands, wiggle fingers, and
lower arms to simulate falling rain.)
And the five little flowers
Lift up their heads again!
(Hold up five fingers.)

Ten little pumpkins

Ten little pumpkins all in a line;
   (Hold up ten fingers.)
One became a Jack-O'-Lantern,
Then there were nine.
   (Bend down one finger.)
Nine little pumpkins peeping through the gate;
An old witch took one,
Then there were eight.
   (Bend down one finger.)
Eight little pumpkins (there never were eleven);
A green goblin took one,
Then there were seven.
   (Bend down one finger.)
Seven little pumpkins full of jolly tricks;
A white ghost took one,
Then there were six.
   (Bend down one finger.)
Six little pumpkins glad to be alive;
A black cat took one,
Then there were five.
   (Bend down one finger.)

Five little pumpkins by the barn door;
A tawny owl took one,
Then there were four.
   (Bend down one finger.)
Four little pumpkins, as you can plainly see;
One became a pumpkin pie,
Then there were three.
   (Bend down one finger.)
Three little pumpkins feeling very blue;
One rolled far, far away,
Then there were two.
   (Bend down one finger.)
Two little pumpkins alone in the sun;
One said, "So long,"
And then there was one.
   (Bend down one finger.)
One little pumpkin left all alone;
A little boy chose him,
Then there were none.
   (Bend down last finger.)
Ten little pumpkins in a patch so green
Made everyone happy on Halloween!

Four big Jack-O'-Lanterns

Four big Jack-O'-Lanterns made a funny sight
Sitting on a gatepost on Halloween night.
Number one said, "I see a witch's hat!"
Number two said, "I see a big, black cat!"
Number three said, "I see a scary ghost!"
Number four said, "By that other post!"
Four big jack-o'-lanterns weren't a bit afraid.
They marched right along in the Halloween parade.
    (Point to one finger at a time.)

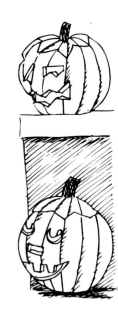

Pumpkin head

My head is round,
    (Make a circle with arms.)
And so are my eyes.
    *(Make circles with thumbs and
    index fingers.)*
My nose is a triangle,
    (Draw a triangle in the air.)
Just this size.
My mouth is turned up
Like a shiny half-moon.
Upon your front porch
I'll be sitting quite soon.
Upon your front porch,
There I will be seen
Smiling at children
    (Children smile; point to smile.)
On this Halloween.

Santa's reindeer

1, 2, 3, 4, 5 little reindeer
    (Pop fingers up one by one.)
Stand beside the gate;
"Hurry, Santa," said the five,
"So we will not be late!"
    (Make fist.)
1, 2, 3, 4, 5 little reindeer;
    (Pop fingers up one by one.)
Santa said, "Please wait!
Wait for three more little reindeer,
And then that will make eight."
    (Hold up three more fingers.)

Making valentines

In February, what shall I do?
I'll make some valentines for you.
The first will have a cupid's face;
The second will be trimmed with lace.
The third will have some roses pink;
The fourth will have a verse in ink.
The fifth will have a ribbon bow;
The sixth will glisten like the snow.
The seventh will have some lines I drew;
The eighth, some flowers—just a few.
The ninth will have three little birds;
The tenth will have three little words:
I LOVE YOU!
    (Point to one finger at a time.)

Five little valentines

One little valentine said, "I love you."
    (Hold up fist; extend one finger.)
Tommy made another; then there were two.
    (Extend another finger.)
Two little valentines, one for me;
Mary made another; then there were three.
    (Extend another finger.)
Three little valentines said, "We need one more."
Johnny made another; then there were four.
    (Extend another finger.)
Four little valentines, one more to arrive;
Susan made another; then there were five.
    (Extend another finger.)
Five little valentines all ready to say,
"Be my valentine on this happy day."

How many valentines?

Valentines, valentines;
How many do you see?
Valentines, valentines;
Count them with me:
    One for Father,
        (Hold up thumb.)
    One for Mother,
        (Hold up index finger.)
    One for Grandma, too;
        (Hold up middle finger.)
    One for Sister,
        (Hold up ring finger.)
    One for Brother,
        (Hold up little finger.)
    And here is one for YOU!
(Make heart shape with thumbs
 and index fingers.)

I had an Easter Bunny

I had an Easter Bunny.
  (Hold up one finger.)
One day she ran away.
I looked for her by moonlight.
  (Hand shading eyes.)
I looked for her by day.
I found her in the meadow
With her babies 1, 2, 3.
  (Point to one finger at a time.)
So now I have four rabbit pets
  (Hold up four fingers.)
To run and jump with me.

Five little Easter eggs

Five little Easter eggs lovely colours wore;
  (Hold up five fingers.)
Mother ate the blue one, then there were four.
  (Bend down one finger.)
Four little Easter eggs, two and two, you see;
Daddy ate the red one, then there were three.
  (Bend down one finger.)
Three little Easter eggs; before I knew,
Sister ate the yellow one, then there were two.
  (Bend down one finger.)
Two little Easter eggs, oh, what fun!
Brother ate the purple one, then there was one.
  (Bend down one finger.)
One little Easter egg, see me run!
I ate the very last one, and then there were none.
  (Bend down last finger.)

Easter rabbits

Five little Easter rabbits
  (Hold up five fingers.)
Sitting by the door;
One hopped away, and then there
were four.
  (Bend down one finger.)

Refrain
  Hop, hop, hop, hop;
    (Clap on each hop.)
  See how they run!
  Hop, hop, hop, hop;
    (Clap on each hop.)
  They think it is great fun!

Four little Easter rabbits
  (Hold up four fingers.)
Under a tree;
One hopped away, and then there
were three.
  (Bend down one finger.)
Repeat refrain.

Three little Easter rabbits
  (Hold up three fingers.)
Looking at you;
One hopped away, and then there
were two.
  (Bend down one finger.)
Repeat refrain.

Two little Easter rabbits
  (Hold up two fingers.)
Resting in the sun;
One hopped away, and there was one.
  (Bend down one finger.)
Repeat refrain.

One little Easter rabbit
Left all alone;
He hopped away, and then there
were none.
  (Hand behind back.)

Refrain
  Hop, hop, hop, hop!
    (Clap on each hop.)
  All gone away!
  Hop, hop, hop, hop!
    (Clap on each hop.)
  They'll come back some day.
    —Unknown

Two little houses

Two little houses closed up tight;
   (Two closed fists.)
Open up the windows and let in the light.
   (Spread hands apart.)
Ten little people tall and straight,
   (Hold up ten fingers.)
Ready for the bus at half past eight!
   (Fingers make running motion.)
      —Unknown

This little cricket

The first little cricket played a violin.
The second little cricket joined right in.
The third little cricket made a crackly song.
The fourth little cricket helped him along.
The fifth little cricket cried, "Crick-crick-cree.
The orchestra is over and it's time for tea!"
   (Point to one finger at a time.)

Little ants

One little ant, two little ants,
Three little ants I see.
Four little ants, five little ants,
Lively as can be.
Six little ants, seven little ants,
Eight in a bowl of glass.
Nine little ants, ten little ants
Entertain our class.
   *(Show the required number of
   fingers each time.)*

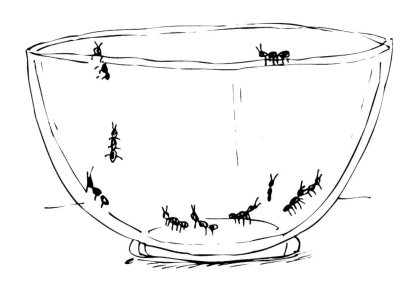

Five little busy bees

Five little busy bees on a day so sunny;
  (Hold up one hand, fingers extended.)
Number one said, "I'd like to make some honey."
  (Bend down first finger.)
Number two said, "Tell me, where shall it be?"
  (Bend down second finger.)
Number three said, "In the old honey-tree."
  (Bend down third finger.)
Number four said, "Let's gather pollen sweet."
  (Bend down fourth finger.)
Number five said, "Let's take it on our feet."
  (Bend down thumb.)
So the five little bees went buzzing along,
Humming their busy little honeybee song.
ZZZZZZZZZZZZZZZZZZZZZZZZZZZ!

Once I saw a beehive

Once I saw a beehive
  (Cup hands together to form hive.)
Out in the maple tree.
I said, "Little honeybees,
Come out and play with me!"
"Bzzzzzz!" went the honeybees
Inside the hive;
  (Motion of peeping inside hive.)
And then they came out—
One, two, three, four, five!
  (Show one finger at a time.)

The little caterpillars

Ten little caterpillars crawled up on a vine.
One slipped off and out of sight, and then there were _____.

Nine little caterpillars sat upon the gate.
One hid behind the latch, and then there were _____.

Eight little caterpillars in a row quite even.
One went to find a leaf, and then there were _____.

Seven little caterpillars tried to find some sticks.
One went behind a bush, and then there were _____.

Six little caterpillars crawled down the drive.
One skittled far away, and then there were _____.

Five little caterpillars were creeping as before.
One slipped inside a crack and then there were _____.

Four little caterpillars climbed up a tree.
One hid behind some bark, and then there were _____.

Three little caterpillars found leaves that were new.
One crawled far out of sight and then there were _____.

Two little caterpillars were snoozing in the sun.
One woke up and dashed away, and then there was _____.

One little caterpillar, before the set of sun,
Turned into a butterfly and then there were _____.
  (The children hold up the required number of fingers
  and supply the remaining number each time.)

The ladybirds

Tick-tack-tick-tack! See them go!
Four little ladybirds are marching in a row.
    (Hold up four fingers.)
The first one is yellow and trimmed with specks of black.
    (Point to one finger at a time.)
The second one is orange with a round and shiny back.
The third one is bright red with teeny, tiny dots.
The fourth one is fancy with different kinds of spots.
Ladybirds are helpful. Ladybirds eat pests.
They eat up all the greenfly,
So our gardens look their best.

Counting ladybirds

One, two, three, four, five,
    (Point to one finger at a time.)
Five little ladybirds walk down the drive.
Their coats are shiny and bright as stars.
They look like small, newly-painted cars.
One, two, three, four, five,
Five little ladybirds walk down the drive.

Ten little grasshoppers

Ten little grasshoppers swinging on a vine;
   (Hold up hands, fingers extended.)
One ate too many berries and then there were nine.
   (Bend down one finger.)

Nine little grasshoppers sitting on the gate;
One was blown away and then there were eight.
   (Bend down one finger.)

Eight little grasshoppers flying toward heaven;
One got lost upon a cloud and then there were seven.
   (Bend down one finger.)

Seven little grasshoppers lived between two bricks;
One said, "I'll hop away," and then there were six.
   (Bend down one finger.)

Six little grasshoppers glad to be alive;
One chased a bumblebee and then there were five.
   (Bend down one finger.)

Five little grasshoppers jumping on the floor;
One hid inside a crack and then there were four.
   (Bend down one finger.)

Four little grasshoppers saw a tiny flea;
One tried to chase it and then there were three.
   (Bend down one finger.)

Three little grasshoppers, and what did they do?
One skipped merrily away and then there were two.
   (Bend down one finger.)

Two little grasshoppers dancing in the sun;
One hid behind a tree and then there was one.
   (Bend down one finger.)

One little grasshopper, left all alone,
Hopped over the grass and then there were none.
   (Make fist.)
   (The children may supply the remaining number each time.)

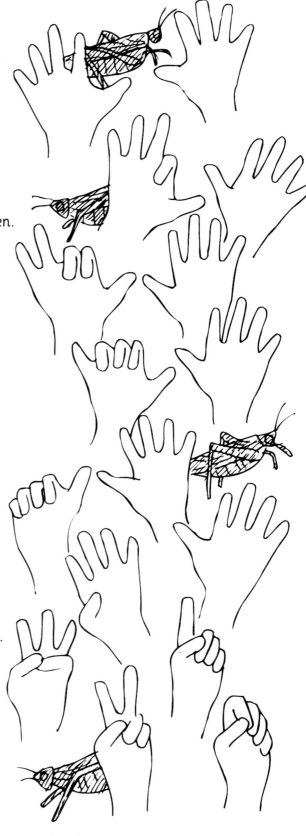

Finger fun

One little finger wiggles in the sun.
Two little fingers run, run, run!
Three little fingers spread wide apart.
Four little fingers point to your heart.
Five little fingers walk up the hill.
Six little fingers stand straight and still.
Seven little fingers climb up a tree.
Eight little fingers fly like a bee.
Nine little fingers scratch in the sand.
All little fingers hide in my hand.
   (Children follow actions of the rhyme.)

Fingers and toes

I have ten fingers,
  (Hold up fingers.)
I have ten toes.
  (Point to feet.)
They help very much as everyone knows!
I do not wish to have fins like a fish,
  (Motion of swimming.)
Or paws like a dog,
  (Double up fists.)
Or webs like a frog,
  (Spread hands.)
Or claws like a bear,
  (Curve fingers into claws.)
Or hooves like a mare,
  (Double up fists, move fists up and down.)
Or scales like a snake,
Make no mistake!
I have ten fingers,
  (Repeat motions.)

I have ten toes.
They help very much as everyone knows!
My fingers feel,
They can turn a wheel.
  (Turn hand around.)
They can hold a cat,
  (Cradle arms.)
Hit a ball with a bat.
  (Hold imaginary bat with two hands.)
My toes like the sand,
And they help me to stand.
My toes can tiptoe,
And wade in the snow.
I have ten fingers,
  (Hold up fingers.)
I have ten toes.
  (Point to feet.)
They help very much as everyone knows!

Five little fire fighters

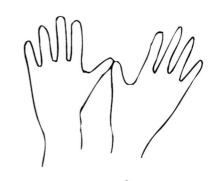

Five little fire fighters sit very still
  (Hold up five fingers.)
Until they see a fire on top of the hill;
Number one rings the bell, ding-dong;
  (Bend down thumb.)
Number two pulls his big boots on;
  (Bend down index finger.)
Number three jumps on the fire engine red;
  (Bend down middle finger.)
Number four puts a fire hat on her head;
  (Bend down ring finger.)
Number five drives the red fire engine to the fire,
  (Bend down little finger.)
As the big yellow flames go higher and higher.
  (Spread arms.)
Whooooo-ooooo! Whooooo-ooooo! hear the fire engine say,
  (Imitate siren.)
As all of the cars get out of the way.
Shhhhh! goes the water from the fire hose spout,
  (Rub palms together.)
And quicker than a wink the fire is out!
  (Clap hands.)

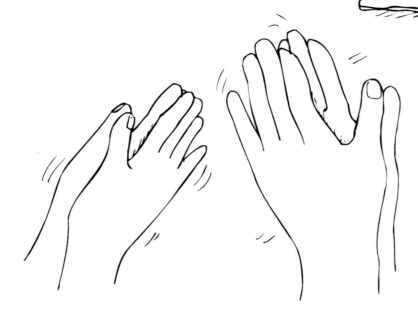

Four busy fire fighters

Four busy fire fighters could not retire
   (Hold up four fingers.)
Because they might have to put out a fire.
The first one rang a big brass bell.
   (Point to one finger at a time.)
The second one said, "It's the Grand Hotel!"
The third one said, "Down the pole we'll slide."
The fourth one said, "Get ready to ride."
The siren said, "Get out of the way!
We have to put out a fire today!"
The red fire engine sped on to the fire,
As the big yellow flames grew higher and higher.
   (Spread arms.)
Swish went the water from the fire hose spout,
And in no time at all, the fire was out.
   (Rub palms together.)
The people all clapped and they gave a big yell:
"The fire fighters saved our Grand Hotel!"
   (Children may dramatize the rhyme.)

The dentist

When I try to count my teeth,
  (Point to teeth.)
I count and count and then,
I have to rest; I've done my best,
I counted up to ten.
One, two, three, four, five, six, seven,
  (Children point to teeth and count.)
Eight, nine, ten.
I then go to the dentist
And let her see my teeth.
  (Open mouth.)
She pumps the chair up to my size
With a pedal underneath.
Up and down the pedal goes,
  *(Raise hand up and down
  several times.)*

And so I take a ride.
And then I open up my mouth
  (Open mouth.)
So she can see inside.
She says to me, "Well, one, two, three,
  (Count on fingers.)
Four, five, six, seven, and eight.
It all looks fine except
Four teeth that must look straight."
  (Hold up four fingers.)
  *(Ask: What will happen to the four teeth
  that are not straight, but crooked? Have
  they ever known anyone to wear
  braces.)*

Ten clerks

One clerk works hard unpacking beans and rice.
Two clerks work hard arranging all the spice.
Three clerks work hard wrapping yellow cheese.
Four clerks work hard sorting drinks and teas.
Five clerks work hard marking all the jam.
Six clerks work hard slicing up the ham.
Seven clerks work hard packaging the sweets.
Eight clerks work hard selling all the meats.
Nine clerks work hard shelving rolls and bread.
Ten clerks worn out go home to bed.
  (Show the correct number of fingers each time.)

Telephone line workers

Over the towns and countryside
Telephone wires stretch far and wide.
   (Hands measure width.)
This first line worker climbs a pole
   (Motion of climbing with hands.)
With bravery and self-control.
The second wears goggles on his eyes
   (Fingers encircle eyes.)
In case some steel from wire flies.
The third one wears a belt with pride.
   (Circle waist with two hands.)
A safety belt is her best guide.
The fourth one climbs in cold and heat
With safe, strong climbers on both feet.
   (Show feet one at a time.)
The fifth, a telephone installs
Just so that you can make your calls.
   (Hand to ear.)
   (This rhyme may be used as a finger
   play to review ordinal numbers.)

Wiggling puppies

One little puppy, one
Wiggled his tail and had wiggling fun.
   (Wiggle finger.)
Two little puppies, two
Wiggled their bodies as puppies do.
   (Wiggle whole self.)
Three little puppies, three
Wiggled their noses happily.
   (Move nose.)
Four little puppies, four
Wiggled their shoulders and wiggled some more.
   (Move shoulders.)
Five little puppies fat and round,
Wiggled their ears when they heard a sound.
   (Choose five children who join the group, one at
   a time, as the rhyme is dramatized.)

Five little puppies

Five little puppies were playing in the sun;
   (Hold up hand, fingers extended.)
This one saw a rabbit, and he began to run;
   (Bend down first finger.)
This one saw a butterfly, and he began to race;
   (Bend down second finger.)
This one saw a pussy cat, and he began to chase;
   (Bend down third finger.)
This one tried to catch his tail, and he went round and round;
   (Bend down fourth finger.)
This one was so quiet, he never made a sound.
   (Bend down thumb.)

One little Kitten, one

One little kitten, one
   (Hold up one finger.)
Said, "Let's have some fun!"
Two little kittens, two
   (Hold up two fingers.)
Said, "What shall we do?"
Three little kittens, three
   (Hold up three fingers.)
Said, "Let's climb up that tree."
Four little kittens, four
   (Hold up four fingers.)
Said, "Let's hide behind the door."
Five little kittens, five
   (Hold up five fingers.)
Said, "Here's a beehive!"
   (Make a fist with other hand.)
"Bzzzzzzzzz" went the bee,
And they scampered up a tree!
   (Move fingers in running motion.)

Little Kittens

Five little kittens playing on the floor;
   (Hold up five fingers.)
One smelled a mouse; then there were four.
Four little kittens, fat as fat could be;
   (Hold up four fingers.)
One saw a puppy; then there were three.
Three little kittens watched how birdies flew;
   (Hold up three fingers.)
One ran far up the tree; then there were two.
Two little kittens snoozing in the sun;
   (Hold up two fingers.)
One chased a rabbit; then there was one.
One little kitten looking for some fun;
   (Hold up one finger.)
He fluffed his tail and scampered off;
Now there isn't even ONE!

Six little fish

Six little fish, two in each pair,
    (Hold up two fingers.)
Coming up occasionally for a breath of air.
Two swim up, and two swim down;
    (Wiggle fingers.)
They swim in a circle around and around.
    (Draw a circle.)
Six come up.
They swim in threes.
But whenever I feed them, they don't say please.
Six little fish swim around, around.
They play tag with each other
And never make a sound.

Goldfish pets

One little goldfish
Lives in a bowl.
Two little goldfish
Eat their food whole.
Three little goldfish
Swim all around.
Where ever they move,
They never make a sound.
Four little goldfish
Have swishy tails.
Five little goldfish
Have pretty scales.
    (Show the correct number of
    fingers each time.)

Fred and his fishes

Fred had a fishbowl.
In it was a fish,
   (Hold up one finger.)
Swimming around with a swish, swish, swish!
Fred said, "I know what I will do.
I'll buy another and that will make _____."
   (Children supply number and hold up two fingers.)
Fred said, "I am sure it would be
Very, very nice if I just had _____."
   (Children supply number and hold up
   three fingers.)
Fred said, "If I just had one more,
That would make one, two, three, _____."
   (Children supply number and hold up
   four fingers.)
Fred said, "What fun to see them dive,
One, two, three, four, _____."
   (Children supply number and hold up five fingers.)
How many fishes do you see?
How many fishes? Count them with me!
   (Children count to five.)
   (Repeat rhyme with a different child's name.)

My pets

There are a lot of pets in my house.
I have one gerbil and one white mouse.
   (Hold up one finger on each hand.)
I have two kittens and two green frogs.
   (Hold up two fingers on each hand.)
I have three goldfish and three big dogs.
   (Hold up three fingers on each hand.)
Some folks say that is a lot!
Tell how many pets I've got.
   (Twelve.)
   (You may make tally marks on the chalkboard
   for the numbers of pets and at the end of the
   rhyme children count them.)

Five little seashells

Five little seashells lying on the shore;
   (Hold up five fingers.)
Swish! went the waves, and then there were four.
   (Show the action; bend down one finger.)
Four little seashells cozy as could be;
Swish! went the waves, and then there were three.
   (Show the action; hold up three fingers.)
Three little seashells all pearly new;
Swish! went the waves, and then there were two.
   (Show the action; hold up two fingers.)
Two little seashells sleeping in the sun;
Swish! went the waves, and then there was one.
   (Show the action; hold up one finger.)
One little seashell left all alone
Whispered "Shhhhhhhh" as I took it home.
   (Bend down last finger.)

Five big waves

I went to visit the beach one day,
And I saw five waves begin to play.
The first wave gave a great big swish!
The second wave washed up several fish.
The third wave washed away my boat,
And there I saw it was afloat.
The fourth wave washed away a shell.
The fifth wave made a little swell.
The five waves played with me all day,
And suddenly, they went away.
   (This rhyme can be used as a finger play or acted out.)

Ten white seagulls

Ten white seagulls
  (Hold up ten fingers.)
Just see them fly
  (Motion of flying.)
Over the mountain,
And up to the sky.
  (Raise arms high.)
Ten white seagulls
  (Repeat motion.)
On a bright day,
Pretty white seagulls,
Fly, fly away!
  (A small group "fly" around the room.)

Octopus, octopus

Octopus, octopus down in the sea,
How many arms can you show to me?
Only one, or will it be two?
  (Show one finger, then two.)
Why are all of these arms on you?
Will it be three or will it be four?
  (Show three, then four fingers.)
Oh, dear me! Are there really more?
Will it be five or will it be six?
  (Show five, then six fingers.)
I think that my eyes are playing tricks.
Will it be seven or will it be eight?
  (Show seven, then eight fingers.)
Tell me, octopus. I cannot wait.
Octopus, octopus, down in the sea,
How many arms can you show me?
"I have eight arms, as you can see."
  (Show eight fingers.)

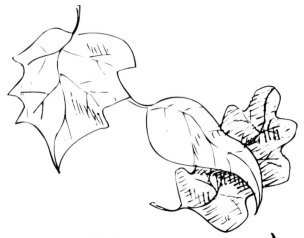

Fall leaves

One leaf and two leaves
Tumbling to the ground,
Three leaves and four leaves
Make a rustling sound.
Five leaves and six leaves
Twirling all around,
Seven leaves and eight leaves
Whirling in a mound.
Nine leaves and ten leaves—
A north wind comes along,
And blows every leaf away
And that ends my song!
*(The children hold up the required
number of fingers each time.)*

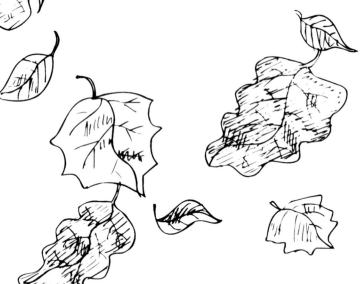

Three little oak leaves

Three little oak leaves, red, brown, and gold,
Were happy when the wind turned cold.
(Hold up three fingers.)
The first one said, "I'll be a coat for an elf;
He'll be able to warm himself."
(Point to first finger.)
The second one said, "I'll be a home for a bug,
So he will be cozy and snug."
(Point to second finger.)
The third one said, "To a tiny seed I'll bring
A coat to keep it warm till spring."
(Point to third finger.)
Three little oak leaves, red, brown, and gold,
Were happy when the wind turned cold.
(Make motions for falling leaves.)

Our tenth month

Wear a warm coat for autumn is here.
It is the tenth month of the year.
    (Hold up ten fingers.)
One for the cornfield,
    (Hold up one finger.)
Two for the leaves,
    (Hold up two fingers.)
Three for the cold rain that drips from the eaves.
    (Hold up three fingers.)
Four for the ponds that soon will freeze,
    (Hold up four fingers.)
And five for empty birds' nests in the trees.
    (Hold up five fingers.)
Wear a warm coat for autumn is here.
It is the tenth month of the year.
    (Hold up ten fingers.)

The three crows

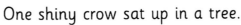

One shiny crow sat up in a tree.
Caw, caw, caw!
Two shiny crows were as fat as could be.
Caw, caw, caw!
Three shiny crows ate from early morn.
Caw, caw, caw!
They ate every ear of the farmer's fresh corn.
Caw, caw, caw!
The scarecrow danced, and they all flew away.
Caw, caw, caw!
And said they would come back again the next day.
Caw, caw, caw!
    (Children hold up one finger at a time to represent the crows. The entire class says the refrain.)

Ten little snowpeople

One little, two little, three little snowpeople,
(Extend three fingers, one at a time.)
Four little, five little, six little snowpeople,
(Extend three more fingers, one at a time.)
Seven little, eight little, nine little snowpeople,
(Extend three more fingers, one at a time.)
Ten little snowpeople bright.
(Extend tenth finger.)

Ten little, nine little, eight little snowpeople,
(Bend down three fingers, one at a time.)
Seven little, six little, five little snowpeople,
(Bend down three fingers, one at a time.)
Four little, three little, two little snowpeople,
(Bend down three fingers, one at a time.)
One little snowperson bright.
(Bend down last finger.)

Snowflakes in our town

The clouds are dark and in our town,
The flakes of snow are falling down.
One, two, three—they're falling fast.
(Hold up three fingers.)
Four, five, six—they'll never last.
(Hold up six fingers.)
Seven, eight, nine—they are so cold.
(Hold up nine fingers.)
Ten, eleven, twelve—all I can hold.
(Hold up ten fingers; stop and hold up two more.)
But, oh, here comes the happy sun!
They're melting!—twelve, eleven, ten, nine,
(Count backward.)
Eight, seven, six, five, four, three, two, one!

Spring is here!

Spring is here! Spring is here!
(Clap four times.)
Winter is gone and two flowers appear.
(Hold up two fingers.)
Three little robins begin to sing.
(Hold up three fingers.)
Four bicycle bells begin to ring.
(Hold up four fingers.)
Five children come out and skip with rope.
(Hold up five fingers.)
Spring is here now! I hope, I hope!

Five little May baskets

Five little May baskets waiting by the door;
(Hold up five fingers.)
One will go to Mrs. Smith, then there will be four.
(Bend down one finger.)

Four little May baskets, pretty as can be;
One will go to Mrs. Brown, then there will be three.
(Bend down one finger.)

Three little May baskets, one is pink and blue;
It will go to Mr. Jones, then there will be two.
(Bend down one finger.)

Two little May baskets, yellow as the sun;
One will go to Mr. Black, then there will be one.
(Bend down one finger.)

One little May basket; oh, it's sure to go
To my own dear mother, who's the nicest one I know.
(Cup hands to form basket.)

Draw a circle

Draw a circle, draw a circle,
Round as can be;
   (Draw a circle in the air with index finger.)
Draw a circle, draw a circle
Just for me.

Draw a square, draw a square,
   (Draw a square in the air.)
Shaped like a door;
Draw a square, draw a square
With corners four.

Draw a triangle, draw a triangle
   (Draw a triangle in the air.)
With corners three;
Draw a triangle, draw a triangle
Just for me.

Let's make a ball

A little ball,
   *(Make a circle with index finger and
   thumb.)*
A bigger ball,
   *(Make a circle with both index fingers
   and thumbs.)*
A great big ball I see;
   (Make large circle with arms.)
Now, let's count the balls we've made;
1, 2, 3.
   (Repeat actions of first three lines.)
   —Traditional

Fingers, fingers

Fingers, fingers everywhere,
Fingers drawing little squares,
Fingers drawing circles round,
Fingers drawing without a sound.
Fingers drawing rectangles,
Fingers drawing little bangles,
Fingers learning how to snap,
Fingers help hands clap, clap, clap!

> *(Children draw shapes suggested in the*
> *air. Weave fingers for bangles, then give*
> *snaps and claps.)*

Leaf buds in March

Ten little leaf buds grew upon a tree,
  (Hold up ten fingers.)
Curled up tightly as little buds should be.
  (Make two fists.)
Now the little leaf buds are keeping snug and warm,
All through the winter weather and the storm.
  (Wave hands back and forth.)
Along comes the cold and the windy month of March,
His breath is icy and it is strong and harsh.
He swings the little leaf buds very roughly, so,
  (Swing arms back and forth vigorously.)
Then very, very gently, he moves them to and fro.
  (Same arm movements, except slowly.)
Until the little raindrops fall down from the skies,
  (Raise arms and let moving fingers fall.)
And make the little leaf buds open up their eyes.
  *(Make two fists and let one finger at a
  time pop out to show ten buds.)*

The nut tree

Five brown chestnuts fell from the tree.
  (Hold up five fingers.)
I thought that the chestnuts were only for me.
But one was taken home by a girl.
  (Hold up four fingers.)
And one was taken home by a squirrel.
  (Hold up three fingers.)
A small brown mouse took one to her nest.
  (Hold up two fingers.)
I hurried up and took all the rest.
  (Hold up one finger.)
I planted one nearby, you see.
Someday, we'll have a new nut tree!
  (Raise arm high.)

Ten little tugboats

Ten little tugboats are out on the sea
And that is where little tugboats should be.

Ten little tugboats got along fine,
Till one drifted far away, and then there were _____.

Nine little tugboats said, "We can't wait."
One went too far out, and then there were _____.

Eight little tugboats were lined up quite even.
One couldn't keep the pace, and then there were _____.

Seven little tugboats, before you could say "ticks,"
One got lost in the fog and then there were _____.

Six little tugboats had a lot of drive.
But one tooted out to sea, and then there were _____.

Five little tugboats said, "Let's move to shore."
But one backed up from the rest, and then there were _____.

Four little tugboats were sailing evenly.
One hit a big barge, and then there were _____.

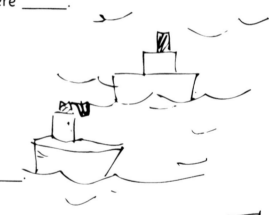

Three little tugboats said, "We'll carry through."
But one lost its engine, and then there were _____.

Two little tugboats said, "We'll make the run."
But one lost its smokestack, and then there was _____.

One little tugboat pulled a ship to shore.
That tugboat was successful, and now there are no more.

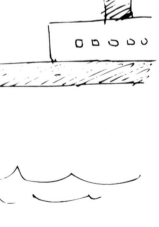

Puddles

One puddle, two puddles
Made by the rain.
Three puddles, four puddles
Down in the lane.
Five puddles, six puddles
We can wade through.
Seven puddles, eight puddles
Quite muddy, too!
Nine puddles, ten puddles
Covering tiny roots.
Eleven puddles, twelve puddles—
We all need our boots.

*(Have twelve children represent puddles. Each
one stands when number is called.)*

Little white clouds

One little white cloud
   (Hold up one finger.)
Played tag in the breeze.
Two little white clouds
   (Hold up two fingers.)
Looked down at the trees.
Three little white clouds said,
   (Hold up three fingers.)
"Hi!" to a plane.
Four little white clouds smiled
   (Hold up four fingers.)
And greeted a train.
Five little white clouds
   (Hold up five fingers.)
Turned to dark grey,
And began to cry on the earth today.
   (Raise fingers in air and lower them gently.)